FOLK TALES of INDIA

THE Traveller THE Tiger AND THE Very Clever Jackal

Written by Reshma Sapre
Illustrated by Jessica Lian

A Hathi Chiti Book

HarperCollins *Children's* Books | **Mapin Publishing**

Long ago, in a small village in India, there lived an old traveller named Raaheeji.

Raaheeji had grown tired of sitting around everyday, dreaming of his old adventures. He decided he would get up early one morning and sneak off on a new adventure.

He got up very quietly, while his old wife lay sleeping. He knew his wife would be very upset to see him go as she told him everyday, "If you leave on another adventure, old man, you may never find your way back to your comfortable home."

With his small bundle slung over his shoulder, Raaheeji walked for miles and miles going nowhere in particular. He left the road and was walking deep in the jungle when he came upon an unusual sight. There, in the middle of the jungle, sat an old Tiger, trapped in an even older cage.

The old man watched as the Tiger tried desperately to get out of his cage. He tried to cut the bars with his big sharp teeth. He tried to unlatch the door with his claws. He even tried squeezing his body through the bars to escape. He tried many different ways to get out, but each time, he would only fall to the floor and get more and more tired and unhappy.

After a while, the Tiger became frustrated and he sat down to lick his tired paws. He turned and suddenly noticed old Raaheeji watching him, and he began to beg and plead. "Oh please, dear traveller, sir, would you please let me out of this cage?" Raaheeji was shocked and delighted because he had never before spoken with a Tiger.

"I would like to help you, my friend," Raaheeji replied, "but I am afraid to. After all, you are a ferocious man-eating Tiger."

"I have been trapped in this cage for so long that I only wish to be free! If you let me out, I would be so grateful to you. Oh, dear traveller, please let me out!" said the Tiger.

"Are you sure that you will not eat me if I open the cage?" asked Raaheeji. He was scared, but he felt sorry for the sad old Tiger begging from the cage.

"My friend, I promise not to eat you! I only wish to be a free old Tiger, living out my days in the jungle."

Raaheeji, being an old man himself, understood the Tiger's request very well. He decided he would help the old Tiger after all.

Raaheeji slowly crept up to the cage and asked the Tiger to stand back. He trembled so much as he undid the latch that he had to use his free hand to hold his other hand in place. The impatient Tiger growled for him to hurry.

The old Tiger didn't even wait for Raaheeji to move aside, he leapt out of the cage, and quickly turned on Raaheeji. "There, I have let you free, now you keep your vow." Raaheeji pleaded. But the Tiger prowled around him, pacing back and forth, looking hungrier and hungrier.

Finally the Tiger spoke. "Old fool, you know that I am a man-eating Tiger, I cannot change what I am; I must eat you."

Raaheeji pleaded in vain for his life, "But you made a vow which you must not break!"

The Tiger thought about this, and finally made a deal with the trusting old man. "Since you have given me a chance," said the Tiger, "I will give you one as well. You want to live and I want to eat you, so we must ask three strangers what they think. And you must promise to do what they decide." The old Tiger knew that no one would help such a foolish old man.

Raaheeji agreed and quickly ran off in search of his three rescuers. As he grew more and more tired during his search, he decided to rest under a Banyan tree and he begged out loud for someone to help him. "Oh what shall I do? How could I be so stupid?" On hearing this, the Banyan tree asked, "Well, what did you do that is so stupid?"

Raaheeji jumped to his feet in alarm, for he had never spoken to a tree before. He told his sad tale to the old Banyan, who thought it over.

"Hmmm," said the Banyan, "you are a foolish old man, but you should be grateful that you are not me. I give everyone shade from the hot sun and shelter from the rain and still they break off my branches to feed their animals. They take from me but they give me nothing in return. As I suffer, so shall you suffer. Go, and face your foolish fate."

As Raaheeji walked away from the Banyan tree, he could not help but think of his old wife. She was right. This would be his last adventure.

He stopped at a well to drink some water and calm himself. When he looked up, his eyes met the two big brown eyes of a mighty Buffalo. The Buffalo was turning the wheel of the well. Raaheeji hoped that the Buffalo would take pity on him and save him from the Tiger's hungry jaws, so he told the Buffalo his tale.

After hearing Raaheeji's story, the Buffalo could only laugh. "Ha ha! You are such a fool," cried the Buffalo, "You expect me to feel sorry for you? Look at me! There was a time when they would feed me lots of food in exchange for my milk. But now that I no longer have milk to give, they have chained me to this well and barely even give me scraps to eat. As I suffer, so shall you suffer. Go, face your foolish fate."

Crying the biggest tears he'd ever cried, Raaheeji began to walk along the road that led back to the Tiger. His tears fell freely on the narrow dirt road and made little puddles on his path. The Road cried out, "It is raining, I shall be washed away!"

Raaheeji looked down and said, "No, you will not. These are just the tears of an old fool. They will dry shortly and I shall be gone for good." Then he had a thought, "Now here is my last chance to save myself." He explained his story to the Road.

"My dear friend, I feel sorry that you are such a fool! I am a pitiful Road. When the rains come, I am washed away. When it is hot and dry, I am trampled on and trash is thrown on me. You've already lived a better life than mine. As I suffer, so shall you suffer. Go, face your foolish fate."

Now, all hope lost, Raaheeji continued on his way back to the Tiger. He was so sad that he did not notice a Jackal walking along behind him.

"My, my, old man," said the Jackal, "Why do you look so sad? You look as miserable as a fish out of water." Old Raaheeji told the Jackal about everything that had happened to him since his fateful meeting with the Tiger.

After he finished telling his story, the Jackal wrinkled his forehead. "My, that's a very confusing story. I'm sorry, but I didn't understand all of it. I got it all mixed up. Please, Raaheeji, please tell me the story again. I don't understand why a Banyan tree wants to eat you?

"No, no, you've got it all wrong, the Tiger in the cage wants to eat me!" cried Raaheeji.

"How can he eat you if he's in a cage?" asked the Jackal, with a confused look on his face.

Once again Raaheeji tried to explain the whole story. and again, the Jackal interrupted.

"I'm sorry, old Raaheeji, but I am having trouble understanding all that has happened. Maybe if you take me to the place where your story began, I'll be able to help you."

So Raaheeji and the Jackal continued on the path towards the cage and the hungry, waiting Tiger.

The Tiger was walking in short circles around his cage. He remembered how hungry he was when he saw old Raaheeji walking towards him. "Well, did you keep our deal, what did the three strangers say? Am I to eat you or not?" He roared when he saw the Jackal. "Who have you brought with you? I will eat both of you, old fool!"

Raaheeji let out a nervous laugh and almost fell over from shaking. The Jackal interrupted the Tiger and said, "You are an old wise Tiger, but I am just a simple Jackal. I am having trouble making a decision. Can you explain what has happened so that I may understand?"

This time, the Tiger began to tell the Jackal the whole story all over again. Once again, with a confused look on his face, the Jackal interrupted the Tiger. "This is surely a confusing tale. My poor, poor head hurts! Wait a minute! Let me see if I understand you. You say that you found the old traveller in a cage–"

"No, no! Foolish Jackal! The old man wasn't in the cage! I was in the cage!" The Tiger roared louder than he ever had before.

"That's silly, you are not in the cage, you are standing right in front of me, and I am not in the cage," said the Jackal as he tried to understand.

"What foolishness! I shall eat you both!" growled the Tiger, growing more impatient.

"Oh dear, perhaps you can just show me what happened," the Jackal said, "I do not know how a Tiger gets into a cage." While he was saying this, old Raaheeji started to open the cage door.

"What do you mean you do not know how a Tiger gets into a cage?" demanded the Tiger. And as he said this, he began to climb into the cage. "See, this is how a Tiger gets into a cage, you fool!"

Just at that moment, Raaheeji slammed the cage door shut and quickly latched it. The Tiger let out a loud cry, "You have fooled me! Once again I am a prisoner of this cage!"

The Jackal looked at Raaheeji and said, "Well, old friend, I have made my decision, you shall not be anyone's dinner today! And next time you see a Tiger in a cage, do not set him free."

Raaheeji thanked the very clever Jackal and said, "Not to worry my friend, for I am returning to my wife and my village, where I shall happily spend the rest of my days!"

First published in India in 2007
by Mapin Publishing
in association with
HarperCollins *Children's* Books,
an imprint of HarperCollins *Publishers* India
a joint venture with The India Today Group

Mapin Publishing Pvt. Ltd.
10B Vidyanagar Society I
Usmanpura, Ahmedabad 380014 INDIA
T: 91 79 2754 5390/91
F: 2754 5392
E: mapin@mapinpub.com
www.mapinpub.com

HarperCollins *Publishers*
1A Hamilton House, Connaught Place, New Delhi
110001, India
77-85 Fulham Palace Road, London W6 8JB,
United Kingdom
Hazelton Lanes, 55 Avenue Road, Suite 2900,
Toronto, Ontario M5R 3L2
and 1995 Markham Road, Scarborough, Ontario
M1E 5M8, Canada
25 Ryde Road, Pymble, Sydney, NSW 2073,
Australia
31 View Road, Glenfield, Auckland 10, New Zealand
10 East 53rd Street, New York NY 10022, USA
www.harpercollins.co.in

Concept by Hathi Chiti
PO Box 3473
New York, NY 10163
E: hathichiti@gmail.com
www.hathichiti.com

Text © Reshma Sapre
Illustrations © Jayme Robinson

ISBN: 978-81-88204-85-4 (Mapin)
ISBN: 978-81-7223-700-4 (HarperCollins *Children's* Books)

Typeset in Bossa Nova
Edited and designed by Hathi Chiti
Printed and bound at
Gopsons Papers Ltd., Noida